This book is a gift to:

Rose
_____

From:

Charlie Raub
_____

Date:

12/09/21
_____

The Blessing Gifts

God's Gifts that transform you to walk in His Calling and Presence

Revealed in the Names
of Jacob's Sons

14 days, 15 gifts

Charley Raub

No part of this book may be reproduced or transmitted in any form or by any means, electronic or mechanical, including photocopying, recording or by any information storage and retrieval system, without written permission from the author.

The information provided within this eBook is for general informational purposes only. While we try to keep the information up-to-date and correct, there are no representations or warranties, express or implied, about the completeness, accuracy, reliability, suitability or availability with respect to the information, products, services, or related graphics contained in this eBook for any purpose. Any use of this information is at your own risk.

The author has made every effort to ensure the accuracy of the information within this book was correct at time of publication. The author does not assume and hereby disclaims any liability to any party for any loss, damage, or disruption caused by errors or omissions, whether such errors or omissions result from accident, negligence, or any other cause.

©2021 by Charley Raub
All Rights Reserved.

ISBN 9798519232289

This devotional study is dedicated in gratitude to my compassionate and amazing wife. Karen, you make all things beautiful. Thank you from my heart for your transforming love.

This book would not exist without the help and encouragement from the following dear friends:

Stephanie Bailey, MD, MS, writer and speaker. Stephanie is the one who prompted me to write down my thoughts concerning the names of Jacob's sons. Then she provided wonderful suggestions and edits. **Glen Roachelle**, president of Gate Ministries and author. Glen gave me valuable suggestions how to update and clarify the manuscript. **Karen Raub**, DTh, teacher, mother and wife extraordinaire. Karen never stopped encouraging me. She helped me rewrite, simplify, and she provided fresh ideas. **Jack Dunigan**, writer of books and blogs, Leadership Trainer for the Navajo Reservation, Principal Owner of 'The Practical Leader.' Jack graciously offered to walk me through ALL the steps from rewriting & editing, to publishing. He has edited, made invaluable suggestions, formatted, etc., and has so sweetly put up with my ignorance in these matters. Thank you, **Michael Gragg** for the classic pine branch graphics.

Contents

Day 1:   Blessing Gift: Beholding Jesus!   3

Day 2:   Blessing Gift: Hearing and being
heard by God   9

Day 3:   Blessing Gift: Being joined to
Christ and His Body   15

Day 4:   Blessing Gift: The power of praise   21

Day 5:   Blessing Gift: Bringing justice
and reconciliation   27

Day 6:   Blessing Gift: Dethroning false
mindsets   33

Day 7:   Blessing Gift: Being in the
evangelistic army of God   39

Day 8:   Blessing Gift: Negatives turn into
happy outcomes   45

Day 9:	Blessing Gift: God rewards overcomers	51
Day 10:	Blessing Gift: Knowing that God dwells in us	57
Day 11:	Blessing Gift: The Lord will add Grace upon Grace	63
Day 12:	Blessing Gift: The gift of suffering with Jesus	71
	Blessing Gift: Sitting with Christ under His authority	71
Day 13:	Blessing Gift: Forgetting injustices by forgiving	77
Day 14:	Blessing Gift: Bearing fruit for Christ and posterity	81
	Postscript	87

This fourteen-day devotional study came about as I reread in Genesis the genealogical list of Jacob's sons. Out of curiosity I found the English meaning of each name. I discovered a correlation of their birth order names to a more vibrant and authentic walk with Jesus. For example, the first son was named Reuben meaning 'Behold a son!' Our own walk begins by beholding our Savior, the Son of God. Jesus is our greatest Gift and Blessing.

Follow the life of the unloved Leah, mother of six of Jacob's sons. She overcame her pain and difficulties through the blessings and gifts from God. Her legacy impacts us profoundly today.

Each Day we will explore the Blessing Gift discovered in each name. Following each devotional is a prayer suggestion, Scriptures for study and meditation, a question to ponder, and a brief personal testimony.

The Blessing Gifts

God's Gifts that transform you to walk in His Calling and Presence

Revealed in the Names of Jacob's Sons

14 days, 15 gifts

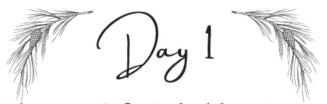

Day 1

Blessing Gift: Beholding Jesus!

Leah was tricked into marrying Jacob, who had worked seven years to marry Rachel, his dream sweetheart. Jacob woke up to find Leah in the wedding bed tent instead of her younger sister Rachel. Jacob, also tricked by his Uncle Laban, had to spend the obligatory wedding week with Leah in order to marry Rachel. Then he had to work yet another seven years for her. It was Rachel he loved so he agreed.

Leah, not beautiful like her sister, was unloved, humiliated, rejected, tricked, and locked in a world of unending disappointment, pain, jealousy, and hopelessness. Just like so many people in the fallen world system we live in today. Maybe just like you. But God had a plan for Leah, and God has a plan for you who are perhaps living in similar circumstances. He saw she was unloved and opened her womb. She gave birth to a son. She called him **REUBEN**, which means **BEHOLD A SON!** "The Lord has looked upon my affliction," said Leah. (She hoped her husband would love her now.)

God's plan had begun to unfold for Leah and her legacy, the birth of the nation of Israel, and our Salvation.

How will your plan unfold? It begins with this: The Son we are to behold.

For unto us a Son is given whose name is Wonderful, Counsellor, the Mighty God, the Everlasting Father, and the Prince of Peace! For God so loved the world he gave His only begotten Son, that whoever believes in Him should not perish but have everlasting life.

God's anchor for the abundant life begins as we behold in all things the Son of God, Jesus. He created the heavens, the earth, and us. He fulfilled the plan of salvation for us; therefore He is the Way to God and the Door to eternal life. He embodies all Truth, and in Him is contained the mystery of Life itself. Shall we then continue to walk in darkness, believing ourselves to know more than God? Shall we trust in politicians, presidents, newscasters, or lose ourselves in drugs, pleasure, or unfiltered entertainment to give us Truth or everlasting life? Absolutely not!

The things that are seen are temporary, the invisible things are eternal; yet God made himself visible to the world through Jesus. Our Lord exhibited the nature of God Himself by healing all manner of diseases, feeding multitudes, setting the bound free, giving sight to the sightless, being a friend to sinners, hating evil and hypocrisy, bringing the dead to life, forgiving sins, and teaching the way to eternal life. But He was mocked, slandered, tortured and crucified. He rose from the dead, and was seen by well over 500 witnesses during a 40 day period. Filled with the Spirit, His followers spread Great News all around the world with joy. They were willing to be martyred to share this greatest of revelations: God lives and loves you; your sins are forgiven. Receive the Gift of eternal Life by beholding the Son, turning to Him for transformation and purpose.

Now just as 'total immersion' is the best way to learn a language, so 'total immersion into Christ, His family, and culture' is the best way to ensure growth as an authentic Child of God.

Prayer: Jesus, I turn my whole being to you for forgiveness and eternal life. You who died on the cross for my sins and rose again from the dead I now receive in trust and faith. You are the Living God who will never leave me as I follow you from this moment on. You are now My Way, My Truth and My Life! Thank you for your Grace and Love.

Scriptures for study and meditation:

Genesis 29: 15-32, Isaiah 9:6-7, John 3:16-17, Colossians 1:13-17, John 14:6, Ephesians 1;17-21, Romans 10:9-10

Question: Am I accountable to Jesus for my behaviors, or do I just agree mentally that what He says is true?

Personal testimony: I was 26 years old, morally broken, feeling rejected and unloved. My emptiness was crushing. A nice apartment and a new car didn't bring me fulfillment. One day, in my deepest emptiness, the Lord entered my living room and spoke, "Turn to me or you will be dead soon." And somehow I knew it meant hell also. I tried to flee His voice as I didn't want to become a Christian. On the third day after hours of struggling in my soul, I gave in and repented of my sins and invited Him to take over my life. Peace flooded in. The next morning the sky was blue, birds were singing, and I was laughing! I picked up a Bible and started reading John and it had become understandable. I was beholding Jesus and He was holding me! The greatest blessing gift is Jesus Himself!

Blessing Gift: Hearing and being heard by God

For Leah, her triumph of producing a male child was tempered by the added dilemma that her sister Rachel now hated her. Leah conceived again and gave birth to another son naming him **SIMEON**. "Because the Lord heard I was hated, He gave me this son," Leah said. Simeon means **HEARING**, or in context **GOD HEARS**.

For us, this next name is significant. The abundant life must include this revelation: God hears our prayers, our hearts, and even what others are saying about us. Best of all He responds. In addition, we learn to hear Him. His sheep know His voice. We learn to discern between our inner voice, the voice of condemnation, and the voice of our past failures versus His Voice of liberation. His Voice is never condemning, but quiet in peace and life giving. Even His correction is given with joy, for it frees us to walk in greater truth and confidence. Our life's walk is dependent on hearing His voice. The written Word becomes alive and speaks to us, as we learn to live in His unconditional love for us.

We freely forgive others because He has forgiven us. As we do so, we are freed from the ravages of a bitter spirit. We learn to heed His Voice. Heed means hearing in deed. Hearing without action is ignoring or even defying Him. There is no close personal relationship with God if we don't do what he says. We walk in agreement with Him. If, for example, He speaks to you to be kind to the foreigner in your land and you turn your back on the foreigner, how can your relationship grow?

God speaks only truth. Truth is the sum of God's attributes. Truth is Jesus Himself. We can speak life or death. If we as Christians argue just to be right, we will end up "*dead* right," destroying relationships and extinguishing our light as believers. Choose to speak life, mercy, and hope to each other.

GOD HEARS our prayers and responds per His good will. Do not think all prayers must be answered. Think of the catastrophes of life if God answered every silly, thoughtless, selfish, or angry prayer. He knows what's best for us to become a Child of light, His delight. Hearing God and heeding is walking in the Spirit. His Voice by the Spirit's leading through the Scriptures, and His Spoken Word to you will always be in agreement.

Prayer: Open my ears and understanding, O God, to hear your voice as I read Your Word; to hear your Heart's desire as I walk to do Your Will. I thank you for listening to my heart's cry and my prayers. Teach me your ways and let me know Your Will, that we may walk together as one.

Scriptures for study and meditation:

Genesis 29: 33, 1 Peter 3:12, 1 John 5:15, John 16:24, Ephesians 4:32, Mark 11:25-26, Psalm 119:105, John 10:27-28, Matthew 12:18-21, Amos 3:3

Question: Do I hear God speaking to me personally?

Personal testimony: As I was standing by a lamp post, I suddenly heard these words: "Honor your father and mother!" I knew it was God speaking. My father had forbidden me to come near his town. No one was allowed to talk to him about me. So, I began by sending him a cordial postcard telling him I had become a Christian and hoped we could reconcile. He wrote back asking what kind of "trip" I was on now. But the lumpy process had begun and after a year we met and came together into a good relationship. All because I heard from God and obeyed. What a blessing gift.

Day 3

Blessing Gift: Being joined to Christ and His Body

Leah gave birth to a third son. Believing that this event would cause her husband Jacob to be joined with her in a closer relationship, Leah named him **LEVI**. Levi means **JOINED** or entwined.

This name speaks of the Levites, the descendants of Levi, who were separated from the other tribes and joined unto GOD, to be priests. When the tribes were given territories in Israel, the Levites weren't given a territory. GOD Himself was the Levites' inheritance! They were scattered throughout Israel to teach the Word, to intercede for the people, to make sacrifices, and to minister to and stand before the Presence of God himself.

In the New Covenant WE all became priests joined to God, ministering to God, interceding for others, and becoming a people separated unto

God Himself. We are collectively joined to Christ as priests, people of prayer, and worshippers.

Before Saul became Paul, he cruelly persecuted Christians. His 'Road to Damascus' experience included Jesus saying, "Saul, Saul, why are you persecuting Me?" This gave Saul the revelation that the Christians were somehow very joined to Jesus Himself. Christians are the Body of Christ on earth, but He is the Head. Join yourself in allegiance to Jesus, not the head of your denomination, a bishop, popular cult, or to a famous celebrity. The Ultimate joining *is* the sealing of The New Covenant with every born again believer through Jesus Christ, who promised to finish the good work He started in each one of us.

Who belongs to this family of Christ?

Jesus explained that whoever does the will of His Father is His brother, sister, and mother. His Church.

Joined to Christ is to be joined to His Word. What we eat becomes part of us. We "eat" the Word, so it will not just be mental assent. This means aligning our thoughts with the Word and walking it. This also means checking out anything that someone tells you as being from God, to find out if Scripture backs it up.

Jesus said, "As I have loved you, so you must love one another. By this everyone will know you are my disciples, if you love one another." Americans' love of being self sufficient and independent has caused a degree of lovelessness and weakness in the communal family of God. The individual believer is often walking independently from the rest of the Body. Church splits easily occur as a result of stubborn quibbling over personal opinions and minor matters. An unteachable spirit cannot relate to or allow a differing viewpoint. An independent person does not see the preciousness of community nor Christ in it.

How can we say we are joined to Christ if we have no love for each other? Does a foot refuse to work together with a leg because of a different function on the same body? Jesus prayed that we would be ONE as He and the father are ONE. We are joined to Christ and thereby joined as the Church. The Church is a worldwide and local community that in the Spirit makes no distinction between male or female, ethnicities or skin color, bosses or workers, rich or poor. Joined to Christ, the Church will see Him working in all things.

❖ ❖ ❖

Prayer: Lord, let me see You as Head of Your glorious Church, Your Body on earth made of reborn, spiritual humans learning to walk in holiness and grace. Let me see your family through Your Eyes: precious, redeemed, beautiful children of the Living God. Let me be forever dependent upon You. Lead me to my place in the Body of Christ. Teach me to pray for others, and lead many to You. Make me a Light for you in this dark world. Mold me into a vessel of honor.

❊ ❊ ❊

Scriptures to study and meditate:

Genesis 29: 34, Deuteronomy 10:8-9, Colossians 1:18-22, Mark 3:31-35, John 13:34-35, 1 John 4:20-21, 1 Corinthians 12:12-25, Acts 17:11

❊ ❊ ❊

Question: Am I actively functioning in the family of God, or am I independent and not contributing?

Personal Testimony: God told me to join a church. Reluctantly I went walking down a street one Sunday and a lady saw me and directed me into a vibrant church. I was ill at ease with how different I was next to all these "together" people. I lifted up my hands and cried to God, "I don't fit here." Suddenly I saw a long rope made of light in the air touching heads, skipping some, landing on others. Then it landed on my head and went into me with this revelation: We all had the same Son, Father, Holy Spirit and Bible! That's what bound us together. I stayed through thick and thin and found my home in my spiritual family.

I was joined to Christ's Body, the Church. What a blessing gift.

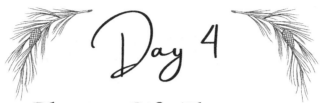

Day 4

Blessing Gift: The power of praise

Leah came to that place where she realized her husband was not going to change, but *she* could. God Himself cared for her! Her focus shifted. As she bore a fourth son, she said, "Now I will praise the LORD." Therefore she called this son **JUDAH** which means **PRAISE**. No longer 'Unloved Leah,' she was 'Triumphant Leah, *Loved by God!*'

The component of praise is our ultimate expression of living in gratitude and freedom. Praise to God morphs quickly into worship and adoration. Praise frees us from focusing on what is wrong in this world to what is right in the heavenly. Praise is a declaration of new found freedom in Christ which infuriates the devil. God dwells in the praises of His people.

As David sang praises on the harp in the court of the King of Israel, evil spirits fled from King Saul.

At the time of King Jehoshaphat, as advancing enemies were approaching, singers were stationed at the front of armies of Judah (the Southern Kingdom of Israel) praising God as per prophetic instructions. The Lord set ambushes and the three armies Judah was facing annihilated each other. All the Israelites had to do was to plunder the dead of their valuables. Praise routed the enemies.

When Paul and Silas, beaten and shackled in jail, began to sing praises at midnight, God answered with an earthquake that broke their shackles and opened the jail doors. Consequently the jailor and his family were brought to salvation by Paul & Silas. Praise sets us free!

When praises erupted as Jesus entered Jerusalem, the Pharisees were threatened and tried to stop it, but couldn't. Spontaneous praise to God is an offense to the proud. Praise unites humble hearts into a glorious chorus of thankfulness and love for God. Praise fills the heavenly spheres. It's the language of Heaven. The morning stars sang together and all the sons of God shouted for joy as the foundations of the earth were laid! Myriads of the redeemed and angels sing praises and worship the Holy God in heaven forever and ever.

❀ ❀ ❀

Prayer: Let gratitude and praise flow from our souls as we look upon the great things You have done, O Lord! Your vast creation, Your endless grace, mercy, and kindness, Your excruciating sacrifice on the Cross to redeem us sinners overwhelms us unto praise! Your constant faithfulness and love are blessings beyond comprehension. May we proclaim your goodness to this world in song and testimony!

❊ ❊ ❊

Scriptures to study and meditate:

Genesis 29:35, Psalm 100, Psalm 22:3, Psalm 148:2, 1 Samuel 16:14-23, 2 Chronicles 20:21-30, Acts 16:16-40, Luke 19: 37-40, Job 38:4-7

❊ ❊ ❊

Question: Am I ruled by my emotions, or do I *choose* to praise God in tough times also?

Personal testimony: One day I woke up feeling negative and very alone. Furthermore my mind provided all sorts of possible depressing scenarios. Out of nowhere the words of an old hymn floated into my head: "Count your blessings, name them one by one." Sarcastically I said, "Okay, thank you, God, for my blender." Then I added spoons, chairs, tables, my apartment, and suddenly I was praising God for friends, salvation, and bringing me out of my depression! Praise works. What a blessing gift!

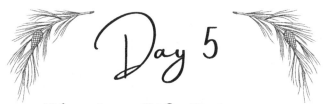

Day 5

Blessing Gift: Bringing justice and reconciliation

RACHAEL, AT THIS TIME childless and envious of her sister, said to Jacob, "Give me children, or else I die!" Jacob became angry and said, "Am I in the place of God who has kept you from birthing children?" She told him that he could produce a baby through her personal maid, Bilhah, that would be birthed between Rachael's knees. That child would be Rachael's via the surrogate mother. She gave Bilhah to Jacob to be his wife. Bilhah bore Jacob a son. Rachael said, "God has judged my case, heard my voice and given me a son." Therefore she called his name **DAN**. The English translation is **JUDGE**.

A prophetic word given by Jacob in his old age to Dan stated, "Dan shall judge his people as one of the tribes of Israel." The judges of Dan provided justice and resolved issues through Godly wisdom and discernment. We are called to be judges: ministers of reconciliation. Called to walk justly. Called to bring the Prince of Peace into hostile situations. Called to be people of discernment and wisdom. Called to bring justice.

God is very clear about our responsibility to take care of the poor, the infirm, the elderly, the widow and the orphan. These are family and church responsibilities, not primarily the government's.

He that is spiritual judges all things. This does not mean condemnation, it means discernment and correct evaluation; an understanding of what needs to be done revealed by the Spirit of God. That spirit was in the sons of Issachar who understood the times and knew what needed to be done. King Solomon also was able to rightly judge situations, expose the truth, and act justly.

Paul was able to rightly judge the condition of a slave girl following his group as she kept shouting, "These men are servants of the Most High God, who show you the way of Salvation!" On the surface this was an accurate, even affirming, statement. After many days of this, Paul cast out this disruptive, mocking spirit of divination. The slave girl lost all her fortune-telling abilities. Because her owners could no longer get money from her fortune telling, they created a riot against Paul. But Paul continued his mission.

Whoever has the Word of God inside him/her in its fullness will grow in ability to judge wisely with compassion and truth.

Prayer: Holy Spirit, make me a minister of reconciliation. Grant me insight, wisdom, and the needed Word of God to judge issues and motives. Let Your Word come to me to resolve issues, expose lies, and bring the Spirit of peace into any situation. Help me draw souls to your Truth and Salvation. Let it be that people will say of me, "This one has been with Jesus to have such wisdom and words of reconciliation!"

Scriptures to study and meditate:

Genesis 30:1-6, Genesis 49:16, James 1:27,
Psalm 82:3-4, Deuteronomy 10:18-19,
2 Corinthians 5:17-21, 1 Corinthians
2:15-16, 1 Chronicles 12:32, 1 Kings 3:7-12,
Acts 16:16-34, Hebrews 4:12, 2 Timothy
3:16-17, Matthew 4:4, James 3:17-18

Question: Do I speak truth lovingly, resolve issues, or do I argue to "win?"

Personal testimony: A group of us were looking for a place for released inmates to live, work, and readjust to life outside prison. A man who identified himself as Christian offered us a ranch with work crew housing. It appeared to be the ideal place for the men to work and live together in a Christian setting. While we were there checking it out, an uneasy feeling came over me. Strong words came to me saying that this man was not a believer, and all he cared about was getting free labor. As soon as we left in our vehicle, one of the group expressed my very thoughts. The rest agreed. Our judgment/discernment of the man later turned out to be true. God had brought judgment to this case, exposing it through discernment. What a blessing gift!

Day 6

Blessing Gift: Dethroning false mindsets

Bilhah conceived again and bore Jacob another son. Rachael said, "With great wrestlings I have wrestled with my sister and have prevailed." She called him **NAPHTALI**, which means **MY WRESTLINGS**. Rachael saw herself in a battle, a wrestling match so to speak, with her sister Leah in an unhealthy competition. The emphasis was '*I* have wrestled and *I* have prevailed.'

Against what do we wrestle today? We don't wrestle against flesh and blood. The war is not against people, but against principalities in high places that put thoughts and concepts into our heads contrary to God's truths. Our battle is to capture and dethrone every ungodly imagination, theory, philosophy, and mindset that keeps us from the knowledge of God and His thoughts. We wrestle against getting locked into the World system which is intent on dethroning God, mocking His people, and installing Man as King. What the world values is control, fame, power, riches, and self worship. The world extols competition, physical beauty, youth, the blame game, sexual expressions outside of marriage, and exacting vengeance. The world worships the earth, celebrities, newscasters, royalty and a materialistic mindset.

But Christ overcame the world!

We now value teamwork, humility, forgiveness, inner beauty, chastity, worshiping God, speaking truth in love, serving others, and training up our children to be Godly men and women with eternal values. We value life and love our enemies. With the knowledge of who we are, we can live free from the world system, for we see the spirit realm. We represent a better society.

We wrestle through prayer and fasting, declaring the Truth of Christ into the atmosphere. In earnest prayer, strongholds and addictions can be broken as we speak freedom and deliverance in Jesus' name for those trapped in darkness. Group prayers have ushered in revivals at various times in various countries. In a revival the once dark spiritual atmosphere becomes clear allowing people a choice for Christ that they were not aware of earlier. People became God conscious.

We wrestle against letting our old sinful nature rule, which wars against the spirit, exerting emotional tyranny, and self-centeredness. But we have been crucified with Christ having died with Him and are also raised up with Him. Therefore, our old sinful life is DEAD. We recognize we have a new nature that is created in righteousness and true holiness! Now in Christ by the indwelling Spirit, we have the power to ignore the callings and pleadings of the flesh, and listen to our new heart and mind. We love walking in victory and newness of life. We love God more than our corrupt old nature. We find pleasure in His Presence and joy sensing His smile. Self-centeredness is dethroned.

The devil has been defeated by Christ. Submit yourselves to God and the devil will flee from you. It is said that Martin Luther saw the devil in his room and, terrified, threw an ink bottle at him inking the wall. Later as Martin grew in maturity, it is said He saw the devil again at his bed and said, "Oh, it's only you!" Turned on his side and went to sleep. Counteract the lies of the enemy with faith in who we are in Christ. Our task is to simply believe the finished work on the cross.

❖ ❖ ❖

Prayer: Father God, let me no longer see myself as a sinner, but as an overcomer. My old selfish nature is forever dead. I am a new eternal creation, forever forgiven. Let me learn to walk boldly in purity and quiet humility, filled with Your love and authority.

❧ ❧ ❧

Scriptures to study and meditate:

Genesis 30:7-8, Ephesians 4:24, 6:12-18,
2 Corinthians 10:3-5, John 16:33,
Matthew 5:44-45, Romans 8:13-14,
Ephesians 4:22-24, Hebrews 2:14-15

❧ ❧ ❧

Question: Am I still in agreement with the philosophies of this anti-Jesus world, or am I free to walk fearlessly with the mind of Christ in this world?

Personal testimony: A great friend, who was saved and baptized at the same time as I, had a cynical buddy who told him it was dumb to believe in an actual devil. Soon my friend received this lie and quit going to church. One evening, at midnight I began to pray fervently for him and suddenly found myself boxing the air with my fists and praying in tongues. I stopped myself. I asked, "Lord is this real? Am I really battling in prayer for my friend, or am I deluded?" Within a few minutes the phone rang. It was my friend. "Charley," he shouted, "I am at work at the convenience store, and suddenly it was like scales fell off my eyes, and I realized there was a God *and* a devil!!!" He returned that Sunday to our fellowship. A false mindset was dethroned! What a blessing gift!

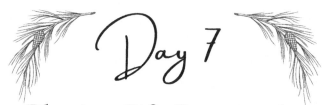

Blessing Gift: Being in the evangelistic army of God

When Leah saw she had stopped bearing, she gave her personal maid, Zilpah, to Jacob as wife. This surrogate mother bore Jacob a son. Leah said, "A troop comes!" and named him **GAD** which means a **TROOP**. [KJV and NKJV translate GAD as TROOP. Other versions say good fortune which is similar to Good News.]

A troop is a group of soldiers. Leah predicted more children would come and in time the armies of Israel resulted from Jacob's sons. Israel was called to be a light to the world; to bring the knowledge of God to the nations. They had only limited success. Also the majority of Jews rejected Jesus as their Messiah. However, there were many Jewish believers in Christ who together with the gentile nations took the Light of the Gospel to the ends of the world. They were clothed not with armor of iron, but with salvation, righteousness, faith, truth and the power of the Spirit. Their Flag? GOOD NEWS! The troops were equipped with signs and wonders, healings, miracles of faith, supernatural words of wisdom and knowledge, casting out of evil spirits, and speaking and interpreting foreign tongues. The Great Commission was in full swing as armies of evangelists made disciples of all the nations, baptizing them in the name of the Father, the Son, and the Holy Spirit, teaching them to do all the things Jesus commanded them. As the evangelists went, Jesus by the Holy Spirit directed them. Multitudes were saved and mentored from Europe to China. Persecution did not stop the troops of joyful evangelists. Sowing in tearful prayers for the lost, they brought in massive harvests of souls. They turned many to righteousness and are still shining like the stars forever. We continue walking in the Great Commission.

Jesus was a friend of sinners. He did not participate in their sins, but He loved them and ate with them and many followed Him. Likewise we want to befriend those outside the church. We are commanded to love our enemies. We befriend those of opposing political parties, viewpoints, and lifestyles. We love them as Christ did. We invite the unsaved into our homes and in time, share our testimonies and scriptures as led by the Spirit. We pray openly with those who are in pain or sick whether in the market or on the golf course. We share how precious communion is with God, and how dreadful it is to die separated eternally without God. We are living sign posts warning of hell, and pointing to Christ who alone rescues, blesses, and rules. We are the troops of God, showing a generation how to regain its identity by restoring the knowledge of their Creator. We restore sonship person by person til there is a collective roar, "We are loved, restored, and awakened by our maker! The emptiness is gone. The fear of death is gone! We are free to love and laugh! Praise the Lord forever and ever!"

Prayer: Holy Spirit, keep me filled with the wonder of my salvation! Let Your call for the lost ever live in my heart. Never let me forget that the horror of eternal separation from God awaits those who choose not to believe. Keep the fear of men from me, for all men die. Help me proclaim the Good News with growing fervor.

Scriptures to study and meditate:

Genesis 30:9-11 NKJ, NKJV only, Matthew 28:18-20, Mark 16:15-20, Acts 1:8, Daniel 12:3, Revelations 12:10-11, 2 Timothy 2:1-4

❧ ❧ ❧

Question: Is sharing my conversion to Christ to others something I see as optional?

_____

_____

_____

_____

_____

_____

_____

_____

_____

_____

_____

_____

_____

_____

_____

_____

_____

_____

_____

Personal testimony: A group of us went periodically to evangelize at a local facility for prisoners. One day as we came into the main hall, Ethel, our leader, said, "Charley, go to the piano and play some upbeat choruses as the men come in." I knew dozens of upbeat contemporary choruses and eagerly sat down to play. My mind went totally blank except for remembering the slow hymn: *The Old Rugged Cross*. I sat trying to remember some happy choruses. "Play!" Ethel shouted. I was going crazy trying to think of any upbeat chorus. I was not going to play that slow hymn. Most of the men were now in the room. "Play *now!*" she shouted again. Turning deep red, I started playing *The Old Rugged Cross*. Suddenly there was a loud shout and one of the men came running to the mike. He excitedly said, "I just asked God that if *He* was real, to make that piano player play *The Old Rugged Cross!!*" My shame and confusion turned to joy and I had the honor of leading him in a sinner's prayer to his salvation! What adventures there are to be had in God's evangelistic army! What a blessing gift!

Day 8

Blessing Gift: Negatives turn into happy outcomes

Leah's maid Zilpah bore Jacob another son. Leah said, "I am happy, for the daughters will call me blessed." So she called his name **ASHER** meaning **HAPPY**. This word connotes blessed, enthusiastic joy.

God is caring and lavish. He dispenses happiness to those who serve Him even in especially distressing situations. The Bible tells us that God has amazingly happy outcomes planned for rejected people. HE gathers the outcasts to himself. To eunuchs (having no possibility of posterity) feeling hopelessly like dried up trees, the Lord said if they followed Him closely, He would give them a place in His House and an everlasting name *better* than that of sons and daughters!!

God grants exceptional faith to the poor.

He sets the solitary in families.

Happy are those who feel insignificant, and

those who are persecuted for righteousness' sake, for theirs is the kingdom of heaven.

The barren woman shall have more (spiritual) children than the married woman.

A man named Caleb, Dog (!) in Hebrew, outlived the 40 years of wandering in the desert. He not only fought during the battle for the promised land, but at the age of 85 asked for the defiant city of Hebron and conquered it!

A woman, bleeding for 12 years, touches the hem of Jesus' garment and is healed.

A bruised reed (= a reed flute) God will not crush. Your restored heart will make melody again.

A smoldering wick God will not put out. Your fire will blaze again.

Ignorant fishermen, a hated tax collector, and a fanatical zealot were chosen by Jesus to be his disciples. They turned the 'world' upside down.

Cornered by mountains, a sea, and the Egyptian army, the Israelites crossed the sea bed on dry land because of the Lord. And what happiness erupted!

HE will wipe away every tear, and everlasting joy shall reign.

Happy is the man whose sins have been washed away.

All things work together for good to those who love God and are called according to His purpose. Happy, blessed are those who put their trust in God.

※ ※ ※

Prayer: God, thank you that all things in time work together for good. Help me rest in this. Let me grow in trust that you are Lord of all, and that Your plans for me are always good. Help me not to grumble or complain, but simply look to You and rest in your Love.

※ ※ ※

Scriptures to study and meditate:

Genesis 30: 12-13, Isaiah 56:3-8, James 2:5, Psalm 68:6, Matthew 5:10-12, Isaiah 54:1, John 14:6-14, Matthew 9:20-22, Isaiah 42:3, Revelations 21:3-5, Romans 8:28

※ ※ ※

Question: Am I negative and a complainer, or am I a happy person because I continuously focus on all of God's past, present, and future blessings?

Personal testimony: With my fresh B.A. degree in German my hopes to be a High School German language teacher were suddenly dashed. High schools no longer offered German. I then had to work 7 years to save enough money to go back to college to earn an elementary school teaching credential. I was disheartened, "What wasted years and setbacks!"

Finally I had a teaching job at an elementary school. Karen, my wife, suggested I spend a few weeks of summer vacation in Germany to attend a Summer Bible School to keep up my German language skills. I went. I became friends with a number of Germans who opened up doors of ministry for me in Europe. In the town of Bad Gandersheim during a quiet prayer time God spoke, "Are you willing to be a father in Albania?" I understood what that meant. I said, "Yes."

I spent three amazing summers with a *Youth With A Mission* team teaching teenagers and young adults in Albania about the Bible and God's love. All my frustrations and negatives of what I thought were wasted years to be a German teacher turned into positives. God turns negatives into happy positives! What a blessing gift!

Blessing Gift: God rewards overcomers

Now Reuben brought his mother Leah mandrakes (also called love apples) he had found. Rachel saw them and asked Leah for some. Leah asked her sister, "Is it a small matter that you have taken away my husband, and now you want my son's mandrakes also?" Rachael bargained successfully to give Leah Jacob for the night in exchange for the mandrakes. Leah conceived and birthed a son naming him **ISSACHAR**. Leah said that God had given her this son as a recompense or a reward for having previously given her maid to Jacob to have children. Apparently this was a heart-rending time to know he was sleeping not only with Rachael but with Zilpah. Her pain and sacrifice was rewarded by God with Issachar, which means **REWARD**.

God has rewards for overcomers, faithful servants of the Lord who make hard decisions for Christ.

He who renounces the doctrines of Balaam (teaching that sexual immorality is okay within the church) and renounces the doctrines of the Nicolaitans (seducing Christians back to 'hip' Roman culture and 'worldly' idol worship) will be given the hidden manna to eat, and a white stone on which is written a new name no one knows except the one receiving it from God.

For faithfulness to the end and overcoming various trials there are five Crowns mentioned as rewards: The Imperishable Crown, The Crown of Rejoicing, the Crown of Righteousness, the Crown of Glory, and the Crown of Life.

Jesus said that everyone who gave up houses or brothers, sisters, father, children for His sake will receive a hundred times as much and will inherit eternal life.

Don't be deceived: if you sow to your flesh you'll reap corruption, but if you sow to the Spirit, you will, by the Spirit, reap everlasting life. So let us not grow weary in doing good, for in due season we shall be rewarded. As we find opportunities, let us do good to all, especially to those of the community of faith.

Jesus, for the JOY set before Him, endured the cross, despised the shame, and sat down at the right hand of the Father. Jesus' reward was the Joy of Glory returning to His Father with His Redeemed!

❖ ❖ ❖

Prayer: Lord, prepare me to overcome temptations and testings by fixing my eyes on Jesus the finisher of my faith. My reward is the joy set before me of eternal fellowship with the Lover of my soul and Redeemer.

❖ ❖ ❖

Scriptures to study and meditate:

Genesis 30:14-18, Revelations 2:10; 2:14-17, 1 Corinthians 9:24-25, 1 Thessalonians 2:19-20, 2 Timothy 4:8, 1 Peter 5:4, Galatians 6:9, Hebrews 12:2, Matthew 19:29

❖ ❖ ❖

Question: Is Jesus my desired reward, or is He just a door to heaven?

Personal testimony: I was really looking forward to attending a concert of Eastern European music which I love. I felt a pull to spend time instead alone with God. I actually fought it off. Then I suddenly decided to give up the concert for Jesus. At the time it seemed like a big decision. After some time in prayer, a simple but beautiful song came to me. I played it on the piano and sang the words from Isaiah. I cried, knowing it was a gift from God for choosing Him over one of my passions. This may seem like a trivial testimony, but God does small special things that are not trivial to the one receiving them. What a blessing gift that God rewards His children who make selfless choices!

Day 10

Blessing Gift: Knowing that God dwells in us

Leah conceived again bearing Jacob a sixth son. She said, God has endowed me with this great gift; now my husband will *dwell* with me, because I have birthed him six sons. So she named him **ZEBULON** which means **HABITATION**. Leah longed for the father of her sons to *dwell* in her tent and not just *visit*.

During the times of the patriarchs and Kings of Israel, the Spirit of God *visited* various men of renown and prophets, coming upon them briefly in power, revelation, or prophetic words. Now, after the Day of Pentecost when the Holy Spirit descended and the Church was birthed, we live in a time of *habitation*. The Holy Spirit dwells in us.

Do you not know that you are the Temple of God and that the Spirit of God lives in you? We are also a collective habitation. In Him we are being built together into a dwelling place for

God by the Spirit. This emphasizes the absolute importance of the family of God to commune with each other in fellowship and not just to visit. Those who feared the Lord spoke to one another, the Lord took notice, and a book of remembrance was written before Him for those who fear Him and esteem His name. Our fellowshipping with each other is recorded. I believe we will get a copy of our own conversations to others about the Lord.

It's one thing to have visitors for a few days. We make sure everything looks good, keeping some rooms closed, and when the visitors leave, we drop back into our comfortable routine. However God has moved permanently into us who are believers. He has a way of going through every room, to clean it, rearrange it, and gently steer our thoughts and desires to match His. A glorious Gentleman, He pours His Love, Words, Concerns, and Goodness into us in such ways, that we say, "Yes, Lord, reign in me for Your ways are so much better and higher than mine! I desire to obey the Lover of my soul." Such communion, peace, freedom, and His leadings bring us to actions that reveal Christ to others signifying: 'It is not I doing this, but Christ in me!'

Prayer: Lord, may the holiness and profound fact of Your Indwelling in me awaken me out of the fog of my earthly perception of myself. I am an adopted child fused with the Creator of the Universe!

❁ ❁ ❁

Scriptures to study and meditate:

Genesis 30:19-20, 1 Corinthians 3:16, Galatians 2:20, Colossians 1:27-29, Hebrews 1:1-4, Malachi 3:16-17

❁ ❁ ❁

Question: Am I willing to let Jesus flow into every room of my life so He can be Lord, or do I deceive myself into thinking I can keep areas for myself and serve two masters?

Personal testimony: I heard this story from a German friend. He had led a young man to the Lord. Just after the young man accepted Christ as his savior, my friend laid his hands on him to receive the Holy Spirit. Becoming seriously quiet the young man said, "I just felt someone enter into me!" This is certainly not everyone's experience, but it illustrates the indwelling of the Spirit of Christ in the believer. Knowing that God lives in us is such a transforming blessing gift!

EXTRA HISTORY

[In Genesis 30:21 we read about the birth of Dinah, the one daughter of Leah. In Genesis chapter 34 we discover Dinah is a tragic figure. She is assaulted by a Hivite prince. Judgment came upon him. Leah's sons Levi and Simeon took vengeance too far and were guilty of the murder of the Prince's countrymen. These events at the time certainly brought extreme grief to Leah. But through God she continued to be an overcomer. Read Genesis 34 for Dinah's story.]

Day 11

Blessing Gift: The Lord will add Grace upon Grace

God listened to Rachael's cry and opened her womb. She also suffered, due to the social stigma of being barren. Now she bore a son and said, "God has taken away my reproach. The Lord will add to me (yet) another son." She named this son **JOSEPH** which means **HE WILL ADD**. Joseph himself was not the titular head of a tribe of Israel. But he had two sons, each of which headed a tribe in Israel. We will discuss them further on. The sons of Joseph are still regarded as sons of Jacob.

The Lord will add. The Lord is lavish. Grace is not only the unmerited favor of God toward us, but Grace also adds the abilities and power we need to accomplish His will as well as provides access to God Himself. We are saved by Grace and are continuously being strengthened by Grace. Grace teaches us to deny ungodliness.

As we draw near to God in prayer we find grace and mercy in times of need. His Grace knows no boundaries. Grace makes up the lack, for God is able to do exceedingly above all that we ask or think! If you lack wisdom He will add it without measure.

Moses said, "If I have found Grace in Your sight, show me Your Glory." And God revealed to His friend His Glory: Kindness, Forgiveness, Goodness, Graciousness, and Compassion!

The Grace of our Lord adds to our souls upgrades in hope, peace, joy, gratitude, love, security, understanding, endurance, kindness, compassion, discernment, godliness, hospitality, generosity, and a glorious future! His Word and Spirit add insight to help us navigate through trials to grow in maturity. When prayers are seemingly not answered, grace imparts to us the added blessing of utter dependence upon God, whose strength is made perfect in our weakness. Certain unhealed disabled people have led thousands to the Lord, for Grace powerfully preaches through their disability.

All the promises in the Bible have been added to give us opportunities to walk in abundant life, to help us withstand the enemy, to give us patience in trials, comfort during sorrow, and joy in all circumstances.

After Joseph's birth, tensions between Jacob and Laban became extremely tense for God had prospered Jacob, and his flocks were more than Laban's. The Lord told Jacob to return to the land of his fathers and family saying that He would be with him. Rachael and Leah united together in agreeing to go. An agreement of peace had been forged between them. Afraid of Laban and his angry sons, they all fled away secretly. Pursued by Laban and his men, the groups confronted each other. But the Lord intervened, preventing bloodshed, and a pact of peace was made. Grace!

Jacob then had more problems. His brother Esau was heading his way. Esau had been tricked out of his birthright and blessings by Jacob decades earlier and there was extreme enmity. Jacob had fled Esau and on the flight had made a promise to God at Bethel saying, "If God will be with me, keep me, give me bread and clothing, and I come back to my father's house, *then* the Lord shall be my God and I will tithe what He gives me."

Jacob, choosing to be alone for a time, fearful of confronting his possibly murderous brother

Esau, suddenly encounters a 'Man' who wrestles with him all night putting Jacob's hip out of joint. Yet Jacob would not let the 'Man' go until He blessed him. He was told, "Your name shall no longer be called Jacob, but Israel; for you have struggled with God and men and have prevailed."

Now Esau was coming with 400 men. Jacob had sent herds of animals ahead as gifts for Esau to appease him. Jacob put his family in a line facing Esau: Zilpah and Bilhah with their children in front, then Leah and her children, and lastly Rachael and Joseph at the end. But Esau ran with enthusiasm toward Jacob and embraced him! He greeted the wives and children in order. By Grace God had provided reconciliation. Eventually Jacob's family reached Bethel. There, Jacob commanded his family to put away all the foreign household gods they had and the earrings of allegiance to them. All the idols were buried. Jacob, now newly named Israel, fulfilled his earlier promises to God. Then God appeared to Jacob and proclaimed that the land given to Abraham was his and that nations and kings would arise from his descendants. Grace upon Grace!

Prayer: Let me live always in the Grace of God, knowing Salvation in Jesus is a finished and complete work. Keep me from slipping into legalism. Keep me aware of the New Covenant in which I am gloriously bound. In my gratitude help me walk in the good works you have ordained for me to bless others!

Scriptures to study and meditate:

Genesis 30:22-24; 35:1-15, John 1:16-17, Ephesians 2:8-10, Ephesians 3:20, James 1:5, 1 Peter 4:8-10, Hebrews 4:15-16, Titus 2:11-12, 2 Timothy 2:1-2, Exodus 33:12-23

Question: Do I really begin to grasp the New Covenant of Grace, and the enormity of complete forgiveness and the lavish Love of God I have been given?

Personal Testimony: Grace comes so often through people. The Grace of God puts people into our lives for us to grow in Him. My Aunt Kathleen and my sister Harriet prayed for my salvation until it happened. Pastor G. gave me balanced teaching and put up with my immaturity. Ethel taught me outreach. Dan taught me to believe I was a new creation when I didn't *feel* like one. Mike taught me, by example, how to share God's love to strangers and pray for them in public. Pastor T. gave me a love for the unlovable. Pastor M. taught me Grace as never before. Karen's love and encouragement for me keeps transforming my selfishness and insecurities into better things. Our daughters, grandkids, and sons-in-law bring us joy beyond belief. I could go on and on. (Forgive me if you don't see your name) Grace upon Grace! What a blessing gift!

Blessing Gift: The gift of suffering with Jesus

Blessing Gift: Sitting with Christ under His authority

Rachael went into severe, hard labor near Bethlehem. As she was dying she birthed a son, calling him **BEN-ONI** meaning **SON OF SORROW**.

But his father called him **BENJAMIN**, or **SON OF MY RIGHT HAND**. Rachel was buried near Bethlehem and Jacob set a pillar on her grave.

These two names point to the life of Jesus as the suffering Son of man, and the triumphant Christ sitting at the Right Hand of the Father. It is in our calling also to suffer and reign with Him. We must acknowledge suffering to be an integral part of fellowshipping with Christ, for it is written that if we suffer with Him, we shall also reign with Him; if we deny Him, He will deny us. He who will be Christ's disciple must deny himself, take up his cross daily and follow Him. We go through many hardships to enter the Kingdom.

There is perhaps no sweeter communion for the believer with Jesus than in suffering. Identifying with His physical and emotional sufferings, rejection, shame and humiliation brings understandings, and closeness not possible by any other means. Combat soldiers have an inkling of this camaraderie as bonds of lasting friendships are formed through suffering together.

Joseph was mocked, hated, threatened with death, betrayed, and sold into slavery by his own brothers. Falsely accused of attempted rape, he was thrown into prison, and forgotten. After suffering thirteen years, he found himself suddenly second in command of all Egypt. He was able to be a just and fair ruler, obviously having empathy for those falsely accused. Through his Seven Year Food Storage program he became a savior of the land of Egypt, neighboring nations, and the families of Israel. After finally reuniting with his brothers in Egypt he forgave them. He preserved the families of Israel (Jacob) giving them the best of the Land of Egypt to dwell in. This is the nature of Jesus in us: forgiving others, serving, bringing healing, salvation; and providing for the needy and the stranger.

God has raised us up with Christ and seated us with Himself in His heavenly realm. We live above our circumstances. We walk carefully as ambassadors of Christ on this earth. As ministers of reconciliation we have authority over the powers of the enemy. Being truly led by the Spirit we can at times bring miraculous healings, cast out evil spirits, and do other miracles because of the authority and will of Christ. Yet we remain always submitted to Jesus as humble Sons and Daughters of the Living God.

One day we will be judging angels. We will be in the armies of heaven arrayed in fine linen, pure and white, following Jesus as He ends the rebellion on earth. Wonderfully, blessed are those who are invited to The Marriage Supper of the Lamb! Let us rejoice and give Him glory, for the marriage of the Lamb has come and the Bride has made herself ready!

Prayer: Father, give me the Grace to embrace the walk that includes suffering for the sweet communion with Jesus and experiencing the preparation of my soul to rule and reign with Him forever.

❧ ❧ ❧

Scriptures to study and meditate:

Genesis 35:16-20, 2 Timothy 2:3-4,12, Acts 14:22, Ephesians 2:6, Luke 10:19, Matthew 10:7-8, I Corinthians 6:2-3, Revelation 19:7-9; 19:13-16

❧ ❧ ❧

Question: Suffering is a precious but painful gift and having authority is a high prize with serious responsibility. Am I willing to finish the race by embracing both?

Personal testimony: We know a remarkable couple in Albania. The woman was a Swiss evangelical midwife ministering in Albania, who also rescued special-needs children from death and misuse. However she was not allowed to take them back with her to Switzerland. She chose to give up comfort and stay in Albania with them. She has suffered much without complaining. For example, she has been through a civil war, protecting her children in the midst of gunfire. Her husband suffered under harsh circumstances as a new believer. He started a church and found himself for years with very little support.

He and his wife now run a beautiful Center to take care of special needs children and adults, as well as pastor their local church. They are blessed and have lifted up Christ faithfully. A section of Albania is under God's favor and authority because of their Light and perseverance. Suffering and reigning with Christ are most precious blessing gifts!

Blessing Gift: Forgetting injustices by forgiving

Joseph was set as administrator over all the land in Egypt at age thirty. Pharaoh gave him the name Zaphnath-Paaneah (= the god speaks and he lives) and gave him an Egyptian bride, Asenath. She gave birth to a son that Joseph named **MANASSEH**, saying, "For God has made me to forget all my hardships, troubles, and my father's house." Manasseh means **CAUSING TO FORGET**.

Joseph had suffered long years serving as a slave and as a prisoner. His faith was tested and in God's timing he was raised up to save his family and nations. How could he forget the past cruelties and betrayals and move on in life? *He forgave.* Forgiveness is what we received from Christ and forgiveness is what we give others. Joseph fully grasped the higher plan behind his life's troubles. He told his fearful brothers (expecting retribution), that though they meant evil for him, GOD had meant this all for good, even for the saving of their own lives. How do we deal with evil that befalls us? We cannot forget the past if we are mired there in bitterness, nor can we move on in life in freedom without forgiveness. Forgiveness frees us from the tyranny of past evil and present bitterness. With trust in God and forgiveness could we ultimately be freed for the saving of many? There is evil in this world. Do we really believe ALL things can work together for good for those who love Christ? If we love Christ we will forgive others. Period. We are not to get stuck in the past, but to live in the moment. Not worrying about tomorrow, we look ahead expectantly at what Christ is about to do.

❧ ❧ ❧

Prayer: Lord, you said on the cross, "Father, forgive them, for they do not know what they are doing." You saw that they truly did *not* know. Let this magnificent other-worldly understanding be in me so that I may forgive likewise.

❧ ❧ ❧

Scriptures to study and meditate:

Genesis: 41:39-51, History: Genesis 37, 39, 40, 41, Genesis 45:1-11; 50:15-21, Ephesians 4:30-32, Matthew 18:21-22; 6:14-15, Colossians 3:12-14, Luke 17:3; 23:34

❉ ❉ ❉

Question: Do I love to continue being a victim for the self righteous anger I get to vent, or do I forgive, move into freedom, take responsibility for the present and future, and grow up?

Personal testimony: For at least 2 years I could not forgive a certain man of the cloth. I said in my head, "I forgive him." But I kept telling others how my wife and I had been unfairly treated. Then I read that I must forgive from my heart. I knew this was huge to God. How can I walk in His forgiveness, if I don't forgive others? One day I even pounded the floor in frustration because I realized my unforgiveness had turned into a weed of bitterness with roots that I couldn't pull out of my heart. I cried, "God, I need you to grant me the ability to forgive." Immediately I saw a vision of the pastor tied up with problems. And he didn't see that he had done any wrong at all. I immediately forgave him. I was free. In time we reconciled easily and became good friends.

I believe injustices sometimes are allowed by God, for it reveals *our* "Love level". If we really love deeply and with understanding we won't easily move into offense. Forgetting injustices by forgiving is a most beautiful blessing gift!

Blessing Gift: Bearing fruit for Christ and posterity

Asenath bore Joseph a second son that he named **EPHRAIM**, saying, "God has caused me to be fruitful in the land of my affliction." The name translates: **FRUITFULNESS**.

Fruitfulness means a life of productivity that benefits others and yourself. It refers to the fruit of the Spirit listed in Galatians as love, joy, peace, long-suffering, kindness, goodness, faithfulness, gentleness, and self control. Fruit grows to mature sweetness by the Spirit. Be patient with yourselves and others. An unripe orange is not yet sweet, though it is a fruit. In time it will mature in sweetness.

Love is the greatest fruit. Love is patient and kind; it does not get envious or parade itself; it is not rude, or selfish; it is not easily provoked, does not think evil of others; does not rejoice at unrighteousness, but rejoices in the truth, bears all things, believes, hopes all things, endures all things and love never quits.

Our salvation does not depend upon our works. But good works are ordained by God, which He prepared in advance for us to do. Fruitful living includes doing those good works that change lives and history. Joseph's life produced fruit that benefited nations, the Jewish people, and our lives today.

Leah's life is not one that many would desire. She was unloved, and stuck in an unhappy marriage triangle, but God saw and cared for her. Raised by a distant, calculating father, in a family that served household gods, she recognized it was the *God of Jacob* who heard her broken heart. *HE* had given her a son! *He* brought her to a place where she found a life of praise and love in Him!

Leah's legacy is astounding! This matriarch gave the nation of Israel six tribes. The tribe of Levi gave us the Levitical Priesthood, Moses, the Ten Commandments, and the first five books of the Bible. The tribe of Judah gave us King David and his psalms, and all the Kings of Judah after David, culminating in the birth of our Messiah and Savior, The Lover of our Souls, **Jesus Himself!!!**

In the Book of Ruth, when Ruth was betrothed to Boaz, the people said a blessing, "The Lord make the woman coming to your house like Rachael and *Leah*, the two who built the house of Israel." Leah remains to this day highly honored in Israel.

As Jacob was dying he asked to be buried in the burial cave of his fathers. Leah, already there, was now together with her husband.

May we walk according to the names of the sons of Jacob in the blessings of each name; trusting that like Leah, our legacy will be richer than our present expectations.

Our God is lavish in goodness toward us. He has given us Blessing Gifts to help us become the Children of God we were designed to be. His plans for us are filled with GLORY!

Prayer: My Saviour, may the fullness of the fruit of the Spirit ever grow to maturity in my soul. May my ways produce salvation in others for a lasting legacy.

Scriptures to study and meditate:

Genesis 41:52, Galatians 5:22-23,
1 Corinthians 13:4-7, Ruth 4:11,
Ephesians 3:20

❧ ❧ ❧

Question: What shall it be? Fleeting fame and approval of men, or a fruitful life walking in peace as a child of God with His approval?

_____

_____

_____

_____

_____

_____

_____

_____

_____

_____

Personal testimony: Any fruit in my life, whether it be the fruit of the Spirit, works of goodness, or legacy has been the product of the workings of the Holy Spirit poured out by Christ Himself. The same is true for you who are reading this.

Almost fifty years ago I was given some verses by the Lord to assure me that *He* would take care of me and bring peace, order, and meaning into my life. Isaiah 54:11 begins: "O you afflicted one, tossed with tempest and not comforted [that was me!], behold I will lay your stones with colorful gems [rebuild me with colorful lasting gems of worth], And lay your foundations with sapphires [blue is the color of Grace: the foundation of my walk for life]. I will make your pinnacles of rubies [towers were for warfare which *He* wages, for red is the color of the Blood of Jesus which defeated the enemy and is the only acceptable Blood for the New Covenant], your gates of crystal [places where decisions are made and proclaimed, where people and ideas are let in or not, shall be clear and transparent as crystal], and all your walls of precious stones [my walls of protection are made of living stones, precious believers, who surround me.] All your children shall be taught of the Lord [whether natural or spiritual children], and great shall be the peace of their children. In righteousness you shall be established [In Christ's Righteousness]

Praise God for the blessing gift of bearing fruit for Christ! What a tremendous blessing gift!!

Postscript

Jacob had twelve sons and one daughter, Dinah. Six sons and Dinah were from Leah; two sons from Zilpah, two sons from Rachael, and two sons from Bilhah. The sons of Leah are underlined.

<u>Levi</u> was a tribe without land other than pasture-lands. Levites were the priests scattered through-out Israel. The 12 tribes as typically pictured on maps are <u>Reuben</u>, <u>Simeon</u>, <u>Judah</u>, <u>Dan</u>, Naph-tali, Gad, Asher, <u>Issachar</u>, Zebulon, Benjamin; Manasseh & Ephraim (both sons of Joseph). Joseph died in Egypt and his two sons' families were counted as two tribes.

Different versions of the Bible give alternate meanings to Jacob's sons' names. Sometimes the Hebrew had several meanings. I chose the meaning that fit the context at the birth scene and/or from the NKJV.

– 87 –

Made in the USA
Monee, IL
02 December 2021

82955866R00056